LAUGH
-OUT-
LOUD
JOKES
for
KIDS

LAUGH -OUT- LOUD JOKES

for KIDS

ROB ELLIOTT

SPIRE

© 2010 by Robert E. Teigen

Published by Revell
a division of Baker Publishing Group
P.O. Box 6287, Grand Rapids, MI 49516-6287
www.revellbooks.com

ISBN 978-0-8007-8803-2

11 12 13 14 15 16 17   14 13 12 11 10 9 8

I'd like to dedicate this book to my wife Joanna,
who I found out is better at coming up with
kids' jokes than I am!

And to

Joshua Bay, Emma Ruth, Leah Rose, and Anna Beth

I want to dedicate this joke book to you because you are some of the greatest joys and blessings that God has given me this side of heaven. I know I've laughed more and smiled more in the years that you've been a part of my life than ever before, so here is a little something to return the favor. Children really are a blessing from the Lord (Psalm 127:3) and I've been blessed beyond what I deserve or ever imagined.

CONTENTS

7

Q & A JOKES

Q: Why did the robber wash his clothes before he ran away with the loot?

A: He wanted to make a clean getaway.

Q: How does a skeleton call his friends?

A: On the tele-bone.

Q: What is the richest kind of air?

A: A millionaire.

Q: Who keeps the ocean clean?

A: The mermaid.

Q: Why did the invisible man turn down a job offer?

A: He just couldn't see himself doing it.

Q: Why did the skeleton drink eight glasses of milk every day?

A: Milk is good for the bones.

Q: Why did Johnny jump up and down before he drank his juice?

A: The carton said to "shake well before drinking."

Q: What is a baby's favorite reptile?

A: A rattlesnake.

Q: **What does a snowman eat for breakfast?**

A: Frosted Flakes.

Q: **Where do generals keep their armies?**

A: In their sleevies.

Q: **How do you make a hot dog stand?**

A: Take away its chair.

Q: **What kind of balls don't bounce?**

A: Eyeballs.

Q: **Why can't you play hide-and-seek with mountains?**

A: Because they're always peaking.

Q: What did the bride say when she dropped her bouquet?

A: "Whoopsy-Daisies."

Q: Why did Jimmy's parents scream when they saw his grades?

A: Because he had a bee on his report card.

Q: What do you call a stick that won't do anything you want?

A: A stick-in-the-mud.

Q: What do you get when you cross a pig and a centipede?

A: Bacon and legs.

Q: What do you get when you cross a tiger and a snowman?

A: Frostbite!

Q: What is a duck on the Fourth of July?

A: A fire-quacker.

Q: Why did the credit card go to jail?

A: It was guilty as charged.

Q: What would we get if we threw all the books in the ocean?

A: A title wave!

Q: What do you call a liar on the phone?

A: A telephony.

Q: What do peanut butter and jelly do around the campfire?

A: They tell toast stories.

Q: What did the baker say when he found the dough he'd lost?

A: "That's just what I kneaded!"

Q: Why did the flashlight, the camera, and the remote-controlled car attend the funeral?

A: They were grieving the dead batteries.

Q: Why wouldn't the team play with the third basketball?

A: Because it was an odd ball.

Q: Where do electric bills like to go on vacation?

A: I-Owe-A (Iowa).

Q: Why did the queen go to the dentist?

A: To get crowns on her teeth.

Q: How did the lobster get to the ocean?

A: By shell-icopter.

Q: When does the road get angry?

A: When someone crosses it.

Q: Why was the king only a foot tall?

A: Because he was a ruler.

Q: What did the robber say when he stole from the bookstore?

A: "I had better book it out of here."

Q: Why did Sally's computer keep sneezing?

A: It had a virus.

Q: When do doctors get mad?

A: When they lose their patients (patience).

Q: **Why did Jimmy throw the clock out the window?**

A: He wanted to see time fly.

Q: **What language does a billboard speak?**

A: Sign language.

Q: **Why didn't the girl trust the ocean?**

A: There was something fishy about it.

Q: **What do you call four bullfighters in quicksand?**

A: Cuatro sinko.

Q: **How did the baseball player lose his house?**

A: He made his home run.

Q: Who was the only person in the Bible without a father?

A: Joshua, because he was the son of Nun (none).

Q: Why did the man put his money in the freezer?

A: He wanted some cold hard cash.

Q: What did the one-dollar bill say to the ten-dollar bill?

A: You don't make any cents (sense).

Q: What happens when race car drivers eat too much?

A: They get Indy-gestion.

Q: Why do baseball pitchers stay away from caves?

A: They don't like bats.

Q: What kind of tree has the best bark?
A: A dogwood.

Q: What kind of makeup do pirate girls wear?
A: Ship gloss.

Q: When do you need Chapstick in the garden?
A: When you're planting the tulips (two lips).

Q: Why did the trees take a nap?
A: For rest (forest).

Q: What is a zucchini's favorite game?
A: Squash.

Q: Why wouldn't the lion eat the clown?
A: He tasted funny.

Q: What kinds of hats do you wear on your legs?

A: Knee caps.

Q: How do you reach a book in an emergency?

A: Call its pager.

Q: Who helped the monster go to the ball?

A: Its scary godmother.

Q: Why did the banana wear sunscreen at the beach?

A: It didn't want to peel.

Q: Where does a ship go when it's not feeling well?

A: To see the dock-tor.

Q: Why was the nose feeling sad?
A: It was tired of getting picked on.

Q: What did the elevator say to its friend?
A: "I think I'm coming down with something."

Q: Why did Billy have a hot dog in his shoe?
A: It was a foot-long.

Q: What gets wet while it dries?
A: A towel.

Q: How did the farmer fix his jeans?
A: With a cabbage patch.

Q: What do you call a silly doorbell?
A: A ding-dong.

Q: What did the sock say to the foot?
A: "Shoe!"

Q: When do you stop at green and go on red?
A: When you're eating a watermelon.

Q: What did one tube of glue say to the other?
A: "Let's stick together."

Q: What did one wall say to the other?
A: "Let's meet at the corner!"

Q: Did you hear about the red ship and blue ship that collided?
A: All the sailors were marooned.

Q: Why did the girl need a ladder to go to school?
A: Because it was high school.

Q: **What do sea monsters eat?**
A: Fish and ships.

Q: **What does a computer do when it's tired?**
A: It crashes.

Q: **What did the tooth fairy use to fix her wand?**
A: Toothpaste.

Q: **Why did the computer get glasses?**
A: To improve his web sight.

Q: **What stays in the corner but travels all over the world?**
A: A stamp.

Q: **What did the computer say when it fell into quicksand?**

A: "Help me! I'm syncing!"

Q: **What do you get when you have two doctors at once?**

A: Pair-a-medics.

Q: **What should you do when you get in a jam?**

A: Grab some bread and peanut butter.

Q: **How can you go surfing in the kitchen?**

A: On a micro-wave.

Q: **Why was everyone looking up at the ceiling and cheering?**

A: They were ceiling fans.

Q: Why did the cowboy go out and buy a wiener dog?

A: Because someone told him to "get a *long*, little doggie."

Q: What is a trombone's favorite playground equipment?

A: The slide.

Q: How can you keep someone in suspense?

A: I'll tell you later.

Q: What happened to the beans when they showed up late to work?

A: They got canned.

Q: Why can't you take anything balloons say seriously?

A: They're always full of hot air.

Q: What happens when you phone a clown three times?

A: You get a three-ring circus.

Q: What do you get when you have breakfast with a centipede?

A: Pancakes and legs.

Q: What do you call someone who is afraid of picnics?

A: A basket case.

Q: How does an Eskimo fix his broken toys?

A: With igloo.

Q: What kind of flowers are great friends?

A: Rose buds.

Q: **What do you get when you cross a tuba, a drum, and a spare tire?**

A: A rubber band.

Q: **Why did the lady sing lullabies to her purse?**

A: She wanted a sleeping bag.

Q: **What did the orange say to the banana when they were looking for the apple?**

A: Keep your eyes peeled.

Q: **Did you hear about the teacher who was cross-eyed?**

A: She couldn't control her pupils.

Q: **What kinds of teeth cost money?**

A: Buck teeth.

Q: What do you call a dentist who cleans an alligator's teeth?

A: Crazy!

Q: If a snake married an undertaker, what would they embroider on their towels?

A: Hiss and Hearse (his and hers).

Q: What is the difference between boogers and broccoli?

A: Kids won't eat their broccoli.

Q: What do elves learn in kindergarten?

A: The elf-abet.

Q: Why did the golfer wear two pairs of pants?

A: In case he got a hole in one.

Q: Why didn't the skeleton go to the ball?

A: He had no body to dance with.

Q: What kind of beans don't grow in a garden?

A: Jelly beans.

Q: Why can't a nose be twelve inches long?

A: If it was, then it would be a foot.

Q: When does your dinner never get hot?

A: When it's chili.

Q: Why did the boys shoot their BB guns in the air?

A: They wanted to shoot the breeze.

Q: Why were the Cheerios scared of the man?

A: He was a cereal killer.

Q: Why did the baseball player go to jail?

A: He stole second base.

Q: Why couldn't the twelve-year-old go to the pirate movie?

A: It was rated arrrgh.

Q: How did Benjamin Franklin feel about discovering electricity?

A: He was shocked.

Q: What do you call cheese that doesn't belong to you?

A: Nacho cheese.

Q: How much did the butcher charge for his venison?

A: A buck.

Q: What does a rain cloud wear under its clothes?

A: Thunderwear.

Q: How did Thomas Edison invent the lightbulb?

A: He got a bright idea.

Q: Why did the lettuce win the race?

A: He was a head.

Q: Where did the most talkative people in the Bible live?

A: Babylon (babble on).

Q: Why was the broom late for school?

A: It over-swept.

Q: What did the alien say to the flower bed?

A: "Take me to your weeder."

Q: What kind of button won't you find at a sewing store?

A: A belly button.

Q: Why did the lady throw her butter out the window?

A: She wanted to see a butterfly.

Q: Why did the ninja go to the doctor?

A: He had kung-flu.

Q: What did the grape do when the lemon asked for a kiss?

A: It puckered up.

Q: Why couldn't the monster go to sleep?

A: It was afraid there were kids under the bed.

Q: How long does it take to count four times infinity?

A: Four-ever.

Q: Who fills your tank at the gas station?

A: Philip (fill up).

Q: What is an alien's favorite kind of candy?

A: A Mars bar.

Q: How do you get a skeleton to laugh out loud?

A: Tickle its funny bone.

Q: What do you take before every meal?

A: You take a seat.

Q: What did the mother corn say to her children?

A: "Don't forget to wash behind your ears."

Q: Did you hear about the actor who fell through the floor?

A: It was just a stage he was going through.

Q: What did the tomato say to the mushroom?

A: "You look like a fungi."

Q: Why are babies so good at basketball?

A: Because they like to dribble.

Teacher: Name two days of the week that start with a "t."

Student: Today and tomorrow.

Teacher: Billy, you missed school yesterday.

Billy: Well, to tell you the truth, I didn't miss it that much at all.

Fred: Today the teacher was yelling at me for something I didn't do.

Mike: What was that?

Fred: My homework.

Q: Why did the cookie complain about feeling sick?

A: He was feeling crummy.

Q: Why is spaghetti the smartest food there is?

A: It always uses its noodle.

Q: What do you call a student who never turns in his math homework on time?

A: A calcu-later.

Q: How did the karate teacher greet his students?

A: "Hi-Yah!"

Q: Why did the bed wear a disguise?

A: It was undercover.

Q: What do you call a boomerang that doesn't come back?

A: A stick.

Q: When do pine trees like to do embroidery?

A: When they do needlepoint.

Q: What is a baby's motto?

A: If at first you don't succeed, cry, cry again.

Q: Where do you keep your jokes?

A: In a giggle box.

Q: Why did the lady wear a helmet every time she ate?

A: She was on a crash diet.

Q: Why did the hot dog turn down the chance to star in a movie?

A: None of the roles (rolls) were good enough.

Josh: Did you hear about the restaurant on the moon?

Anna: What about it?

Josh: It has great food but no atmosphere.

Q: What do you call a fairy that doesn't take a bath?

A: Stinkerbell.

Q: What did one candle say to the other?

A: "Do you want to go out tonight?"

Q: What is a plumber's favorite vegetable?

A: A leek.

Q: How did the French fry propose to the hamburger?

A: He gave her an onion ring.

Q: What has four legs and one head but only one foot?

A: A bed.

Q: What do potatoes wear to bed?

A: Yammies.

Q: What fruit teases people a lot?

A: A bana na na na na na!

Q: Why was the metal wire so upset?

A: It was getting all bent out of shape over nothing.

Q: What do you call the story of the three little pigs?

A: A pigtail.

Q: What did the peanut butter say to the bread?

A: "Quit loafing around."

Q: What did the bread say back to the peanut butter?

A: "I think you're nuts."

Q: What kind of lights did Noah use on the ark?

A: Flood lights.

Q: How did the orange get into the crowded restaurant?

A: He squeezed his way in.

Q: Why can't the bank keep a secret?

A: It has too many tellers.

Q: Why was the sewing machine so funny?

A: It kept everyone in stitches.

Q: Why did the hamburger always lose the race?

A: It could never ketchup.

Q: How do you punish a naughty eyeball?

A: Give it fifty lashes.

Q: Why was the rope so stressed out?

A: It was getting itself all tied in knots.

Q: What did the math book say to the psychiatrist?

A: "Would you like to hear my problems?"

Q: What do you call a fossil that never does any work?

A: A lazy bones.

Q: What did the pen say to the pencil?

A: "You're sure looking sharp today."

Q: What is green and can sing?

A: Elvis Parsley.

Q: Why didn't the string ever win a race?

A: It was always tied.

Q: What is the best food to eat when you're scared?

A: I scream.

Q: How do you get a tissue to dance?

A: Put a little boogie in it.

Q: What did the tree say to the flower?

A: "I'm rooting for you."

Q: What is the craziest way to travel?

A: By loco-motive.

Q: What did the paper say to the pencil?

A: "You've got a good point."

Q: What is the cheapest way to travel?

A: By sale-boat.

Q: Who are the cleanest people in the choir?
A: The soap-ranos.

Q: What is the noisiest game you can play?
A: Racket-ball.

Q: What did the earthquake say to the tornado?
A: "Don't look at me, it's not my fault."

Q: What did the tree say to the lumberjack?
A: "Leaf me alone!"

Q: Why was it so hot in the stadium after the baseball game?
A: All the fans left.

Q: Why did the ice cream cone become a reporter?

A: He wanted to get the scoop.

Q: What did the ice cream cone ride to the store?

A: A fudge-cycle.

Q: What kind of poles can swim?

A: Tadpoles.

Q: Why wouldn't the teddy bear eat anything?

A: He was already stuffed.

Q: How does a gingerbread man make his bed?

A: With a cookie sheet.

Q: What do you get when you cross an elephant with Darth Vader?

A: An ele-Vader.

Q: What do cowboys like on their salad?

A: Ranch dressing.

Q: Why was the elf crying?

A: He stubbed his mistle-toe.

Q: How do you make an orange giggle?

A: Tickle its navel.

Q: What kind of candy is never on time?

A: Choco-late.

Q: What kind of music does a boulder like?

A: Rock-n-roll.

Q: What did the mommy rope say to the baby rope?

A: "Don't be knotty."

Q: What do you call a monster with a high IQ?

A: Frank-Einstein.

Q: What did the turkey say to the ham?

A: "Nice to meat you!"

Q: Why was the Incredible Hulk so good at gardening?

A: He had a green thumb.

Q: What did the pool say to the lake?

A: "Water you doing here?"

Q: **What did the cake say to the knife?**

A: "Do you want a piece of me?"

Q: **What was the math teacher's favorite dessert?**

A: Pi.

Q: **What does bread wear to bed?**

A: Jam-mies.

Q: **Who earns a living driving their customers away?**

A: Taxi drivers.

Q: **What did the lumberjack say to the tree?**

A: "I have an axe to grind with you."

Customer: Excuse me, waiter, but is there spaghetti on the menu?

Waiter: No, but I believe we have some in the kitchen.

Q: What was the best time of day in the Middle Ages?

A: Knight-time.

Q: What is the fastest peanut butter in the world?

A: Jiffy.

Q: Why was the baseball player a bad sport?

A: He stole third base and then went home.

Q: Where do lumberjacks keep their pigs?

A: In their hog cabin.

Q: What is the difference between a football player and a dog?

A: A football player has a whole uniform, but a dog only pants.

Q: Why was the science teacher angry?

A: He was a mad scientist.

Q: Why was the tree excited about the future?

A: It was ready to turn over a new leaf.

Q: What do trees eat for breakfast?

A: Oakmeal.

Q: What is worse than finding a worm in your apple?

A: Finding *half* of a worm in your apple!

Q: Why did Cinderella get kicked out of the soccer game?

A: She ran away from the ball.

Q: What is a race car driver's favorite meal?

A: Fast food.

Q: What does a skipper eat for breakfast?

A: Captain Crunch.

Q: If April showers bring May flowers, what do Mayflowers bring?

A: Pilgrims.

Q: What runs around the football field but never moves?

A: A fence.

Q: Why was the jelly so stressed out?

A: It was spread too thin.

2

AWeSOME ANiMAL JOKeS

Q: A cowboy arrives at the ranch on a Sunday,
stays three days, and leaves on Friday. How is
that possible?

A: The horse's name is Friday.

Q: What do you call a bear standing in the rain?

A: A drizzly bear.

Q: What happened when the spider got a new car?

A: It took it for a spin.

A duck walks into a store and asks the manager if he sells grapes. The manager says no, so the duck leaves. The next day the duck goes back to the store and asks the manager if he sells grapes. The manager says, "NO, we don't sell grapes," so the duck leaves the store. The next day the duck goes back to the same store and asks the manager if he sells grapes. The manager is furious now and says, "NO, WE DO NOT SELL GRAPES! IF YOU COME BACK AND ASK IF WE SELL GRAPES AGAIN, I'LL NAIL YOUR BEAK TO THE FLOOR!" The next day the duck goes back to the same store and says to the manager, "Excuse me, do you sell nails at this store?" The manager says, "No, we don't sell nails." The duck replies, "That's good. Do you sell grapes?"

Q: What do you get from a pampered cow?

A: Spoiled milk.

Q: What is a reptile's favorite movie?
A: The Lizard of Oz.

Q: Why did the cow become an astronaut?
A: So it could walk on the moooo-n.

Q: Where do birds invest their money?
A: In the stork market.

Q: Where do ants like to eat?
A: At a restaur-ant.

Q: Where do shrimp go if they need money?
A: The prawn shop.

Q: Why were the chickens so tired?
A: They were working around the cluck.

Q: Why did the boy canary make the girl canary pay for her own meal on their date?

A: Because he was cheep.

Q: What do cows like to eat?

A: Smoooothies.

Q: Why do flamingos stand on one leg?

A: If they lifted the other leg, they'd fall over.

Q: What do you get when you cross a fish and a kitten?

A: A purr-anha.

Q: What kind of bull doesn't have horns?

A: A bullfrog.

Q: How are fish and music the same?

A: They both have scales.

Q: Why did the skunk have to stay in bed until it felt better?

A: It was the doctor's odors.

Q: What did the mother lion say to her cubs before dinner?

A: "Shall we prey?"

Q: What's worse than raining cats and dogs?

A: Hailing taxi cabs.

Q: Why are pigs so bad at football?

A: They're always hogging the ball.

Q: **What do you call a lion whose car breaks down five miles before he gets to the zoo?**

A: A cab.

Q: **What is a whale's favorite game?**

A: Swallow the leader.

Q: **Why are fish so bad at basketball?**

A: They don't like getting close to the net.

Q: **Where do dogs go if they lose their tails?**

A: The re-tail store.

Q: **What do you call bears with no ears?**

A: B.

Q: Why is it hard to trust what a baby chick is saying?

A: Talk is cheep.

Q: Why did the clown visit the aquarium?

A: To see the clown fish.

Q: What is as big as an elephant but weighs zero pounds?

A: The elephant's shadow.

Q: Why are horses always so negative?

A: They say "neigh" to everything.

Q: What is black and white, black and white, black and white, black and white, splash?

A: A penguin rolling down an iceberg into the water.

Q: What is the smartest animal?

A: A snake, because no one can pull its leg.

Two men went deer hunting. One man asked the other, "Did you ever hunt bear (bare)?" The other hunter said, "No, but one time I went fishing in my shorts."

Q: What is the best way to communicate with a fish?

A: Drop it a line!

Q: Why couldn't the elephants go swimming at the pool?

A: They were always losing their trunks.

Q: Why did the sparrow go to the library?

A: It was looking for bookworms.

Q: What did the dog say when he rubbed sand-paper on his tail?

A: "Ruff, ruff."

Q: What is black and white and red all over?

A: A penguin that's embarrassed.

Q: What do you call a pig that is no fun to be around?

A: A boar.

Q: What kind of fish can perform surgery?

A: Sturgeons.

Q: What kind of sea creature hates all the others?

A: A hermit crab.

Q: **Where can you go to see mummies of cows?**

A: The Mooseum of History.

Q: **What kind of seafood tastes great with peanut butter?**

A: Jellyfish.

Q: **What do you get when you cross a pig and a tree?**

A: A pork-upine.

Q: **What do cats like to put in their milk?**

A: Mice cubes.

Q: **Why is it easy to play tricks on lollipops?**

A: They're suckers.

Q: What do you get when you cross an elephant with a fish?

A: Swimming trunks.

Q: What do you do if your dog steals your spelling homework?

A: Take the words right out of his mouth.

Q: Why did the cat get detention at school?

A: Because he was a cheetah.

Q: Where do bees come from?

A: Stingapore and Beelivia.

Q: Why couldn't the polar bear get along with the penguin?

A: They were polar opposites.

Q: What did the rooster say to the hen?

A: "Don't count your chickens before they hatch."

Q: What did the whale say to the dolphin?

A: "Long time no sea."

Q: What sound do porcupines make when they kiss?

A: "Ouch, ouch."

Q: What happened when the frog's car broke down?

A: It had to be toad away.

Q: What happens when a cat eats a lemon?

A: You get a sourpuss.

Q: What language do pigs speak?

A: Swine language.

Q: What do cars and elephants have in common?

A: They both have trunks.

Q: What is a whale's favorite candy?

A: Blubber gum.

Q: What is a bat's motto?

A: Hang in there.

Q: What do you get when you cross a rabbit and frog?

A: A bunny ribbit.

Q: What do you get when you cross a dog and a daisy?

A: A collie-flower.

Q: What does a cat say when it's surprised?

A: "Me-WOW!"

Q: Why did the parakeet go to the candy store?

A: To get a tweet.

Q: What do you have if your dog can't bark?

A: A hush-puppy.

Q: Why do seagulls fly over the sea?

A: Because if they flew over the bay they'd be bagels.

Q: What do you get when you cross a cow and a rabbit?

A: You get hare in your milk.

Q: Why did the horse keep falling over?

A: It just wasn't stable.

Q: How do fish pay their bills?

A: With sand dollars.

Q: Which creatures on Noah's ark didn't come in pairs?

A: The worms—they came in apples.

Q: How do you shoot a bumblebee?

A: With a bee-bee gun.

Q: Why did Fido beat up Rover?

A: Because Rover was a Boxer.

Q: What do you get when an elephant sneezes?

A: You get out of the way!

Q: What is the craziest bird in the world?

A: The coo-coo bird.

Q: What is the dumbest bird in the world?

A: The do-do bird.

Q: What do you get when your dog makes your breakfast?

A: You get pooched eggs.

Q: Why did the horse wake up with a headache?

A: Because at bedtime he hit the hay.

Q: What do trees and dogs have in common?
A: They both have bark.

Q: Why do bumblebees smell so good?
A: They always wear bee-odorant.

Q: What do you get if you mix a rabbit and a snake?
A: A jump rope.

Q: What do you call a boring dinosaur?
A: A dino-snore.

Q: What is a frog's favorite drink?
A: Croak-a-Cola.

Q: What kind of bees never die?
A: Zom-bees.

Q: **What do you call a lazy kangaroo?**

A: A pouch potato.

Q: **What happened when the sharks raced each other?**

A: They tide (get it . . . they tied).

Q: **Why couldn't the goats get along?**

A: They kept butting heads.

Q: **What type of bat is silly?**

A: A ding-bat.

Q: **Why are frogs so happy?**

A: They just eat whatever bugs them!

Q: What is the difference between a fish and a piano?

A: You can't tuna fish.

Q: What did the horse say when he tripped?

A: "Help! I've fallen and I can't giddy-up."

Q: If people like sandwiches, what do lions like?

A: Man-wiches.

Q: When do fireflies get uptight?

A: When they need to lighten up.

Q: Why do rhinos have so many wrinkles?

A: Because they're so hard to iron.

Q: Where did the turtle fill up his gas tank?

A: At the shell station.

Q: Why did the pony get sent to his room without supper?

A: He wouldn't stop horsing around.

Q: Why did the chicken cross the road?

A: To show the squirrel it could be done.

Q: Why did the turkey cross the road?

A: To prove it wasn't a chicken.

Q: What do you give a horse with a bad cold?

A: Cough stirrup.

Q: Who falls asleep at a bullfight?

A: A bull-dozer.

Q: What is a snake's favorite subject in school?

A: World hiss-tory.

Q: What kind of animal is related to a computer?

A: A ram.

Q: What do you call an insect that complains all the time?

A: A grumble-bee.

Q: Why were the deer, the chipmunk, and the squirrel laughing so hard?

A: Because the owl was a hoot!

Q: Why did the cat and her kittens clean up their mess?

A: They didn't want to litter.

Q: What is a sheep's favorite kind of food?

A: Bah-bah-cue.

Q: What is a hyena's favorite kind of candy?

A: A Snickers bar.

Q: How do sea creatures communicate underwater?

A: With shell phones.

Q: What do you call a monkey who won't behave?

A: A bad-boon.

Q: What kind of bugs read the dictionary?

A: Spelling bees.

Q: What do you call a calf that gets into trouble?

A: Grounded beef.

Q: What do you call a dinosaur who's scared all the time?

A: A nervous Rex.

Q: What do you call a polar bear in Hawaii?

A: Lost!

Q: Why was the dog depressed?

A: Because his life was so ruff.

Q: What does a rabbit use to fix its fur?

A: Hare-spray.

Q: What kind of insect is hard to understand?

A: A mumble-bee.

Q: Where do you take a sick bumblebee?

A: To the wasp-ital.

Q: Who made the fish's wishes come true?

A: Its fairy cod-mother.

Q: Where do pigs go for a rest?

A: To their ham-mock.

Q: What do you call a cow that can't give milk?

A: A milk dud.

Q: Why did the birds get in trouble?

A: They were using fowl language.

Q: Where does a lizard keep his groceries?

A: In the refriger-gator.

Q: Why is talking to cows a waste of time?

A: Whatever you say goes in one ear and out the udder.

Q: What do you get if a cow is in an earthquake?

A: A milkshake.

Q: How does a farmer count his cattle?

A: With a cow-culator.

Q: Why does a milking stool only have three legs?

A: Because the cow has the udder one.

Q: Where do rabbits go after their wedding?

A: They go on their bunny-moon.

Q: What do you get when you cross a dog with a cell phone?

A: A golden receiver.

Q: Where did the bull take the cow on a date?

A: To dinner and a mooovie.

Q: What is the world's hungriest animal?

A: A turkey: it just gobble, gobble, gobbles!

Joe: There were ten cats on a boat and one jumped off. How many were left?

Jack: I don't know, Joe. I guess nine?

Joe: No, there were none! They were all a bunch of copy cats.

Q: How come hyenas are so healthy?

A: Because laughter is the best medicine.

Q: Why don't Dalmatians like to take baths?

A: They don't like to be spotless.

Q: What do you get when sheep do karate?

A: Lamb chops.

Q: What happened to the mouse when he fell into the bathtub?

A: He came out squeaky clean.

Q: When do you ask hamburgers lots of questions?

A: When you want to grill them.

Q: What is a duck's favorite snack?

A: Cheese and quackers.

Q: What do you call a cow that's afraid of everything?

A: A cow-ard.

Q: Why did the rooster go to the doctor?

A: It had the cock-a-doodle-flu.

Q: What do birds do before they work out?

A: They do their worm-ups.

Q: What kind of insects are bad at football?

A: Fumblebees.

Q: What do you call a deer with no eyes?

A: No eye deer (no idea).

Q: Why is it so easy for an elephant to get a job?

A: Because they'll work for peanuts.

Q: What is the difference between a cat and a frog?

A: A cat only has nine lives but a frog croaks every day.

Q: What does a frog say when he washes windows?

A: "Rub it, rub it, rub it."

Q: What do you get when a lion escapes from the zoo?

A: A cat-astrophe.

Q: What is the best kind of cat to have around?

A: A dandy-lion.

Q: What did the tiger say to her cubs when they wanted to go out and play?

A: "Be careful—it's a jungle out there!"

Q: Why did the monkey almost get fired?

A: It took him a while to get into the swing of things.

Q: Why is the snail one of the strongest creatures in the world?

A: They can carry their houses on their backs.

Q: What do you get when you cross a bear with a forest?

A: You get fur trees.

Q: Where do trout keep their money?

A: In a river bank.

Q: What did the worm say to her daughter when she came home late?

A: "Where on earth have you been?"

Q: What did the boy say when he threw a slug across the room?

A: "Man, how slime flies!"

Q: Why did the elephant cross the road?

A: It's an elephant, so who's going to stop him?

Q: What is a frog's favorite flower?

A: A croak-us.

Q: How do you keep a dog from barking in the backseat of the car?

A: Put him in the front seat of the car.

Q: What do you get when you cross a monkey and a peach?

A: You get an ape-ricot.

Q: How do you greet a frog?

A: "Wart's up?"

Q: Who brings kittens for Christmas?

A: Santa Claws.

Q: What did Santa give Rudolph for his upset stomach?

A: Elk-A-Seltzer.

3

Knock Knock Jokes

Knock knock.
  Who's there?
Butter.
  Butter who?
I butter not tell you—it's a secret.

Knock knock.
  Who's there?
Wendy.
  Wendy who?
Wendy you think we'll be done with these knock knock jokes?

Knock knock.
Who's there?
Hailey.
Hailey who?
Hailey a cab so I can go home.

Knock knock.
Who's there?
Wayne.
Wayne who?
The Wayne is really coming down, so open the
door!

Knock knock.
Who's there?
Weasel.
Weasel who?
Weasel be late if you don't hurry up.

Knock knock.
    Who's there?
Norway.
    Norway who?
There is Norway I'm leaving until you open this
    door.

Knock knock.
    Who's there?
Raymond.
    Raymond who?
Raymond me to go to the store to get some milk
    and eggs.

Knock knock.
    Who's there?
Nose.
    Nose who?
I nose a lot more knock knock jokes if you want to
    hear them.

Knock knock.
　　Who's there?
Hannah.
　　Hannah who?
Hannah me some of those apples, I'm hungry!

Knock knock.
　　Who's there?
Little old lady.
　　Little old lady who?
I didn't know you could yodel!

Knock knock.
　　Who's there?
Olive.
　　Olive who?
Olive you. Do you love me too?

Knock knock.
　　Who's there?
Eileen.
　　Eileen who?
I'm so tall, Eileen over to get through the door.

Knock knock.
  Who's there?
Les.
  Les who?
Les cut the small talk and let me in.

Knock knock.
  Who's there?
Brett.
  Brett who?
Brett you don't know who this is!

Knock knock.
  Who's there?
Bacon.
  Bacon who?
I'm bacon a cake for your birthday.

Knock knock.
  Who's there?
Irish.
  Irish who?
Irish you'd let me in.

Knock knock.
  Who's there?
Ashley.
  Ashley who?
Ashley I changed my mind and I don't want to
  come in.

Knock knock.
  Who's there?
Italy.
  Italy who?
Italy a shame if you don't open this door!

Knock knock.
  Who's there?
Alda.
  Alda who?
Alda kids like my knock knock jokes.

Knock knock.
  Who's there?
Gwen.
  Gwen who?
Gwen do you think we can get together?

Knock knock.
   Who's there?
Francis.
   Francis who?
Francis next to Spain.

Knock knock.
   Who's there?
Cook.
   Cook who?
Are you as crazy as you sound?

Knock knock.
   Who's there?
Juno.
   Juno who?
Juno it's me so let me in now!

Knock knock.
   Who's there?
Alex.
   Alex who?
Alex plain later, now let me in!

Knock knock.
  Who's there?
Gladys.
  Gladys who?
Aren't you Gladys is the last knock knock joke?

Knock knock.
  Who's there?
Joanna.
  Joanna who?
Joanna come out and play?

Knock knock.
  Who's there?
Archie.
  Archie who?
Archie going to let me in?

Knock knock.
  Who's there?
Robin.
  Robin who?
Robin a bank is against the law.

Knock knock.
    Who's there?
Duncan.
    Duncan who?
Duncan cookies in milk tastes good.

Knock knock.
    Who's there?
Pastor.
    Pastor who?
Pastor potatoes. I'm hungry!

Knock knock.
    Who's there?
Carson.
    Carson who?
Carson the freeway drive really fast.

Knock knock.
    Who's there?
Ben.
    Ben who?
I've Ben gone a lot lately and came by to see you.

Knock knock.
> Who's there?

Doug.
> Doug who?

I Doug deep and still couldn't find my keys. Please let me in!

Knock knock.
> Who's there?

Aldon.
> Aldon who?

When you're Aldon with dinner can you come out and play?

Knock knock.
> Who's there?

House.
> House who?

House it going for you?

Knock knock.
>Who's there?

Arlo.
>Arlo who?

Arlo temperature is making me cold. Please let me in!

Knock knock.
>Who's there?

Ben.
>Ben who?

I haven't Ben over to visit in a long time.

Knock knock.
>Who's there?

Mia.
>Mia who?

Mia hand is killing me from all this knocking. Will you please let me in?

Knock knock.
Who's there?
Anna.
Anna who?
Anna chance you'll let me in? It's cold out here!

Knock knock.
Who's there?
Samantha.
Samantha who?
Can you give me Samantha to my questions?

Knock knock.
Who's there?
Lee.
Lee who?
I'm lone Lee without you. Please let me in!

Knock knock.
Who's there?
Ya.
Ya who?
Giddyup, cowboy!

Knock knock.
> Who's there?

Cameron.
> Cameron who?

Is the Cameron? I want to take a picture.

Knock knock.
> Who's there?

Stan.
> Stan who?

Stan back because I'm going to break down the
> door!

Knock knock.
> Who's there?

Ice.
> Ice who?

It would be really ice to see you, so please open the
> door.

Knock knock.
Who's there?
Eyes.
Eyes who?
Eyes better come in before I catch a cold.

Knock knock.
Who's there?
Ada.
Ada who?
I Ada lot for lunch so now I'm really full.

Knock knock.
Who's there?
Dewey.
Dewey who?
Dewey have to go to school today?

Knock knock.
Who's there?
Jell-o.
Jell-o who?
Jell-o, it's me again!

Knock knock.
    Who's there?
Peas.
    Peas who?
Peas, can you come out and play?

Knock knock.
    Who's there?
Fanny.
    Fanny who?
If Fanny body asks, I'm not home.

Knock knock.
    Who's there?
Hugo.
    Hugo who?
Hugo first and I'll go second.

Knock knock.
    Who's there?
Megan.
    Megan who?
You're Megan me crazy with all of these knock
    knock jokes.

Knock knock.
  Who's there?
Owen.
  Owen who?
I'm Owen you a lot of money, but I'll pay you back
  soon!

Knock knock.
  Who's there?
Lucas.
  Lucas who?
Lucas in the eye and tell us you don't want to hear
  another knock knock joke!

Knock knock.
  Who's there?
Luke.
  Luke who?
You Luke like you want to hear another knock
  knock joke!

Knock knock.
  Who's there?
Quack.
  Quack who?
You quack me up with all these knock knock jokes.

Knock knock.
  Who's there?
Sadie.
  Sadie who?
If I Sadie magic word will you let me in?

Knock knock.
  Who's there?
Queen.
  Queen who?
I had a bath, so I'm queen as a whistle!

Knock knock.
  Who's there?
Baby Al.
  Baby Al who?
Baby Al will, baby Al won't.

Knock knock.
Who's there?
Canoe.
Canoe who?
Canoe come out and play?

Knock knock.
Who's there?
Oldest.
Oldest who?
Oldest knocking is giving me a headache.

Knock knock.
Who's there?
Woody.
Woody who?
Woody like to hear another knock knock joke?

Knock knock.
Who's there?
B.C.
B.C. who?
I'll B.C.-ing you soon.

Knock knock.
   Who's there?
Weed.
   Weed who?
Weed better go home now for dinner.

Knock knock.
   Who's there?
Dawn.·
   Dawn who?
Dawn mess around, or I'm leaving!

Knock knock.
   Who's there?
Rockefeller.
   Rockefeller who?
Rockefeller in his cradle and he'll go right to sleep.

Knock knock.
   Who's there?
Dora.
   Dora who?
A Dora is between us, so open up!

Knock knock.
Who's there?
Braden.
Braden who?
Are you busy Braden your hair or will you open the door?

Knock knock.
Who's there?
Hannah.
Hannah who?
Hannah over the keys so I can open this door!

Knock knock.
Who's there?
Gary.
Gary who?
Gary me inside—my legs are tired.

Knock knock.
 Who's there?
I don't know.
 I don't know who?
I don't know who either, so open the door and find
 out.

Knock knock.
 Who's there?
Beth.
 Beth who?
I didn't sneeze!

Knock knock.
 Who's there?
Shelby.
 Shelby who?
Shelby coming around the mountain when she
 comes!

Knock knock.
   Who's there?
Howl.
   Howl who?
**Howl we get away from all these knock knock
   jokes?**

Knock knock.
   Who's there?
Water.
   Water who?
Water you doing at my house?

Knock knock.
   Who's there?
Vera.
   Vera who?
Vera few people think these jokes are funny.

Knock knock.
   Who's there?
Garden.
   Garden who?
Stop garden the door and let me in!

Knock knock.
Who's there?
Henrietta.
Henrietta who?
Henrietta bug and now he's sick.

Knock knock.
Who's there?
Annie.
Annie who?
Annie reason you're not opening the door?

Knock knock.
Who's there?
Dozen.
Dozen who?
Dozen anyone ever open the door?

Knock knock.
Who's there?
Dragon.
Dragon who?
These jokes are dragon on and on.

Knock knock.
Who's there?
Willie.
Willie who?
Willie tell us more knock knock jokes?

Knock knock.
Who's there?
Moe.
Moe who?
Moe knock knock jokes, please.

Knock knock.
Who's there?
Ernest.
Ernest who?
Ernest is full of chicken eggs.

Knock knock.
Who's there?
Taylor.
Taylor who?
Taylor brother to pick up his toys.

Knock knock.
    Who's there?
Dewy.
    Dewy who?
Dewy get to hear more knock knock jokes?

Knock knock.
    Who's there?
Lettuce.
    Lettuce who?
Lettuce in and you'll find out.

Knock knock.
    Who's there?
Collette.
    Collette who?
Collette crazy, but I'd like to come in and see you.

Knock knock.
    Who's there?
Radio.
    Radio who?
Radio not, here I come!

Knock knock.
Who's there?
Achoo.
Achoo who?
Achoo my gum every day.

Knock knock.
Who's there?
Juicy.
Juicy who?
Juicy any monsters under my bed?

Knock knock.
Who's there?
Alaska.
Alaska who?
Alaska one more time to let me in!

Knock knock.
Who's there?
Yellow.
Yellow who?
Yellow, and how are you doing today?

Knock knock.
  Who's there?
Doughnut.
  Doughnut who?
Doughnut open the door to strangers!

Knock knock.
  Who's there?
Handsome.
  Handsome who?
Handsome food to me—I'm really hungry!

Knock knock.
  Who's there?
Rabbit.
  Rabbit who?
Rabbit carefully, it's a Christmas present!

Knock knock.
  Who's there?
Sarah.
  Sarah who?
Is Sarah doctor in the house? I feel sick!

Knock knock.
   Who's there?
Ida.
   Ida who?
Ida know, why don't you open up and find out?

Knock knock.
   Who's there?
Oscar.
   Oscar who?
Oscar a silly question, get a silly answer.

Knock knock.
   Who's there?
Dishes.
   Dishes who?
Dishes not the end of my knock knock jokes!

Knock knock.
   Who's there?
Olive.
   Olive who?
Olive these knock knock jokes are making me sick.

Knock knock.
Who's there?
Who.
Who who?
Are you an owl or something?

Knock knock.
Who's there?
Sombrero.
Sombrero who?
Sombrero-ver the rainbow.

Knock knock.
Who's there?
Ken.
Ken who?
Ken you come out and play?

Knock knock.
Who's there?
Itchy.
Itchy who?
Bless you!

Knock knock.
Who's there?
Gorilla.
Gorilla who?
Gorilla me a hamburger—I'm hungry!

Knock knock.
Who's there?
Ivan.
Ivan who?
Ivan to come in, so please open the door!

Knock knock.
Who's there?
Dwayne.
Dwayne who?
Dwayne the bathtub! I'm drowning!

Knock knock.
Who's there?
Walter.
Walter who?
Walter you doing here so early?

Knock knock.
Who's there?
Justin.
Justin who?
You're Justin time for dinner.

Knock knock.
Who's there?
Wanda.
Wanda who?
Do you Wanda let me in yet?

Knock knock.
Who's there?
Rufus.
Rufus who?
Your Rufus on fire!

Knock knock.
Who's there?
Everest.
Everest who?
Do we Everest from telling knock knock jokes?

Knock knock.
Who's there?
Bill Gates.
Bill Gates who?
Bill Gates a bike for his birthday.

Knock knock.
Who's there?
Lion.
Lion who?
Quit lion around and open the door.

Knock knock.
Who's there?
Paws.
Paws who?
Can you paws for a moment and open the door?

Knock knock.
Who's there?
Zoo.
Zoo who?
Zoo think you can come out and play?

Knock knock.
Who's there?
Tide.
Tide who?
Are you Tide of knock knock jokes yet?

Knock knock.
Who's there?
Candace.
Candace who?
Candace be the last knock knock joke?

Knock knock.
Who's there?
Shirley.
Shirley who?
Shirley I'll tell you another knock knock joke.

Knock knock.
Who's there?
Aspen.
Aspen who?
Aspen thinking about you all day.

Knock knock.
    Who's there?
Bonnie.
    Bonnie who?
It's Bonnie long time since I've seen you.

Knock knock.
    Who's there?
Andy.
    Andy who?
Andy-body want to go to the movies?

Knock knock.
    Who's there?
Isabel.
    Isabel who?
Isabel ringing or am I just hearing things?

Knock knock.
    Who's there?
Benjamin.
    Benjamin who?
I've Benjamin to the music all day.

Knock knock.
    Who's there?
Bailey.
    Bailey who?
I know you Bailey know me, but can I come in?

Knock knock.
    Who's there?
Byron.
    Byron who?
There's a Byron get one free sale at the mall!

Knock knock.
    Who's there?
Les.
    Les who?
Les one there is a rotten egg!

Knock knock.
    Who's there?
Baldwin.
    Baldwin who?
You'll be Baldwin you're older.

Knock knock.
    Who's there?
Barry.
    Barry who?
Let's Barry the hatchet and be friends again.

Knock knock.
    Who's there?
Carrie.
    Carrie who?
Will you Carrie my books for me?

Knock knock.
    Who's there?
Calvin.
    Calvin who?
Calvin you get there so I know that you made it
    safely.

Knock knock.
> Who's there?

Colin.
> Colin who?

Just Colin to tell you another great knock knock
joke.

Knock knock.
> Who's there?

Orange.
> Orange who?

Orange you glad it's me?

Knock knock.
> Who's there?

Conner.
> Conner who?

Conner brother come out and play?

Knock knock.
> Who's there?

Jim.
> Jim who?

Jim mind if I come in and stay awhile?

Knock knock.
Who's there?
Mike.
Mike who?
Turn up the Mike so I can hear you better.

TONGUE TWISTERS

Try to Say These Ten Times Fast

Giggly gladiator.

Fresh French fries.

Selfish shellfish.

Sock, skirt, shirt.

Snatch stacked snacks.

Cheap cheese stinks.

Goofy gorillas gobble grapefruits.

Tall trees toss leaves.

Purple penguins pick pickles.

Cooked cookies crumble quickly.

Soggy stuff smells suspicious.

Big bad bears blow blue bubbles.

Tasty tomato tostadas.

You'll push she'll push.

Six slimy snails sailed silently.

Anonymous

A big black bug bit a big black dog
on his big black nose!

by Kitty Morrow

Tongue Twisting Poems

Billy Button

Billy Button bought a buttered biscuit.
Did Billy Button buy a buttered biscuit?
If Billy Button bought a buttered biscuit,
Where's the buttered biscuit Billy Button bought?

by Shirish Karker

A Fly and a Flea in a Flue

A fly and a flea in a flue
Were imprisoned, so what could they do?
Said the fly, "Let us flee!"
"Let us fly!" said the flea,
So they flew through a flaw in the flue.

by Ogden Nash

5

Some Things
To Think About

What do you call a male ladybug?

Why don't they call moustaches mouthbrows?

Why doesn't glue stick to the inside of the bottle?

What do they call their good plates in China?

Why is a boxing ring square?

If a fly didn't have wings, would we call it a walk?

Do fish ever get thirsty?

Rob Elliott has been a publishing professional for more than fifteen years and lives in West Michigan, where in his spare time he enjoys laughing out loud with his wife and four children.